KEY SYSTEM
ALBUM

JIM WALKER

INTERURBANS SPECIAL 68

Library of Congress Catalog Number 78-55027
ISBN: 0-916374-31-9

First Printing: May 1978
Second Printing: March 1980

Interurbans

P.O. Box 6444 Glendale, California 91205

Publisher . . . . Mac Sebree

Editor . . . . Jim Walker

Dust Jacket Photographs

(FRONT) **A TRAIN OF ARTICULATED UNITS** built for use on the San Francisco-Oakland Bay Bridge by the Key System emerges from the Northbrae Tunnel, north of Berkeley, a short distance from the F line terminal at Thousand Oaks, in 1946.
A.R. Alter
(BACK) **CECIL B. DE MILLE'S LATEST CINEMATIC TRIUMPH** still packed them into the Grand Lake Theatre, on Grand Ave. in Oakland, in pre-television 1947, when this No. 12 streetcar passed the movie palace.
Robert T. McVay

End Sheet Photograph

READY FOR ACTION, these shiny new Bridge Units were photographed at the Bridge Yard, at West Oakland, in 1939, the year the rapid transit railway was opened.
Robert S. Ford Collection

Title Page Photograph

OVER HILL AND DALE the Key System's rail network brought fast, efficient transportation to East Bay residents. As it approaches Piedmont, C line extension shuttle car (No. 956, at right) takes leave of trackage it has shared with the No. 10 local car line. In this pre-World War II period, through cars from the Pier went only as far as 41st and Piedmont Ave.
Tom Gray Collection/E.R. Mohr

Introduction

WELCOME to our armchair excursion on the fabled Key System. After publication of our Special 65, RED TRAINS IN THE EAST BAY in 1977, many readers asked: "What about the **other** electric railway on the east shore of San Francisco Bay?" Little has been published on this major electric railway system save for that pioneer historical effort, FROM SHORE TO SHORE, by Vernon J. Sappers. So, we resolved to give you a hefty sample of the Key System in this, our Special 68.

Because noted Bay Area rail historians are well along on a definitive history of the Key System and its predecessors, we have made no attempt in this volume to go beyond a pictorial survey. You will find no car roster and no system map and, outside of the information necessary to caption each photograph, our presentation may leave unanswered many of your questions. These questions, we are confident, will be fully answered in due course when the long-awaited Key System history appears.

Only a few of the fine rail photographers who captured Key on film are represented in our sampling of rail, bus and ferryboat views. We thank all whose photos are contained in this album, and have credited each photo individually. One cautionary note is appropriate: it seems to have been the custom among rail enthusiasts to trade, sell or copy each other's photography. A particular problem is the Magna Collection, because the late Ira L. Swett did not always identify the source of the photos contained therein. We have attempted to trace these and others to give proper credit to the original source and where we have failed, we tender our apologies in advance.

Special thanks to the following persons for additional help: Rudy Brandt, Brian Thompson, Warren K. Miller, Roger Ciapponi, E.R. Mohr, Bob Burrowes, John McKane, Ed Keilty, and Mark Effle.

Jim Walker
April, 1978

"The Key Route"

WE CAN ONLY TOUCH upon the history of this vast Eastbay transit undertaking. The complexities of its corporate structure, the variety of its rolling stock, and the vastness of its routes rank it among one of the most fascinating electric railways of this nation.

Southern Pacific had a near monopoly on the transbay service from the East Bay to San Francisco with its fleet of ferryboats and steam-powered trains. Then came Francis Marion "Borax" Smith, who opened his San Francisco, Oakland & San Jose Railway in 1903. Not only did he give direct competition to many of SP's rail routes, but his newly built trestle and pier jutted out more than three miles into San Francisco Bay and his new ferryboats offered a much shorter voyage to the San Francisco side.

How did the Key System get its name? The name, and the symbol illustrated on the first page came about because it occurred to railway officials early on that, viewed from the air, the long trestle from shore to the mid-Bay Pier resembled to a remarkable degree a door key—one of those old-fashioned kind that used to open up hotel rooms. So . . . before "public relations" was ever called that, the Key System hit upon a fine P.R. device which stamped the system as one of importance and strategic location.

The corporation underwent a number of name changes, and by 1923 its slogan, amended to Key **System**, became the corporate name (Key System Transit Company). In 1929, Railway Equipment and Realty Company was formed to hold the operating properties as subsidiaries: Key System, Ltd. operated the big trains, Key Terminal Railway Ltd. ran the ferryboats and freight service, and Eastbay Street Railways Ltd. and Eastbay Motor Coach Lines, Ltd. managed, respectively, the streetcar and bus lines.

The fifth operation, least-known, was the National Service Company, Ltd. which operated the restaurants, newsstands, checking stands and bootblack stands (and, during the 1939-40 Golden Gate Exposition, the "Elephant Trains").

In all, six transbay lines were built from the Key Pier to Oakland, Piedmont and Berkeley points, and more than 20 streetcar and 16 bus lines were operating by 1930. The Depression hit the Key System hard and streetcar abandonments had cut into the rail system long before the sale, in 1946, of the corporations to National City Lines' interests. This company owned many other transit operations and was noted for its pro-bus policies.

Immediate orders were placed for hundreds of General Motors and Mack diesel buses (both were, at the time, holders of NCL stock) and by November 1948, the last local car lines ceased operation. On April 20, 1958, the final five transbay rail lines, which had operated into San Francisco over the San Francisco-Oakland Bay Bridge since 1939, were converted to bus operation. The remaining all-bus Key System was sold to the Alameda-Contra Costa Transit District on October 1, 1960.

Public transport had suffered because of the shift of many riders to their own automobiles, yet not long after the bridge railway was torn up and the bay bridge was made one-way on each deck to cope with the crush of motorists, the voters of Bay Area counties brought into being the Bay Area Rapid Transit District (BART). It is ironic that many of its route miles parallel or nearly duplicate the Key System routes discarded as being obsolete or "inflexible."

With its 75-mile, high-speed rail network, BART carries on the tradition begun by "Borax" Smith.

LOOKING SOUTH at bucolic San Leandro Plaza (E. 14th and Washington), in 1901, as No. 341 passes a horse and wagon. **Randolph Brandt Collection**

SAN LEANDRO

Predecessors

MANY STREETCAR COMPANIES were formed in the pioneer years of electric railways in the East Bay cities. Among them were the Oakland Consolidated St. Ry., Central Ave. R.R., Alameda, Oakland & Piedmont, Piedmont & Mountain View, the Oakland Railroad, and the Oakland, San Leandro & Haywards Electric R.R. Six had merged by 1898 and the addition of others later tied them together in the early part of the century as the Oakland Traction Company, later the East Bay Street Railways (a division of the Key System empire).

(RIGHT) **THIS SINGLE-TRUCKER** was handsomely striped and lettered in the style of the day.
Mark Effle Collection

ORNATE LETTERING AND STRIPING was common when these cars ran from Oakland to Berkeley. This Oakland Consolidated Street Railway Co. car clearly showed on the letterboard how it was routed between the two communities. A close inspection of the uniforms of the two gentlemen seated inside the car at right discloses that they are from the Salvation Army.
Mark Effle Collection

Key Route Trains

THE ORIGINAL ROLLING STOCK for the San Francisco, Oakland and San Jose Railway was these wooden, railroad-roof electric cars. The Key Route introduced the pantograph current-collection, adopted by rival Southern Pacific when it electrified its own suburban service. This early view shows a conductor standing at each rear step. **A.C. Transit**

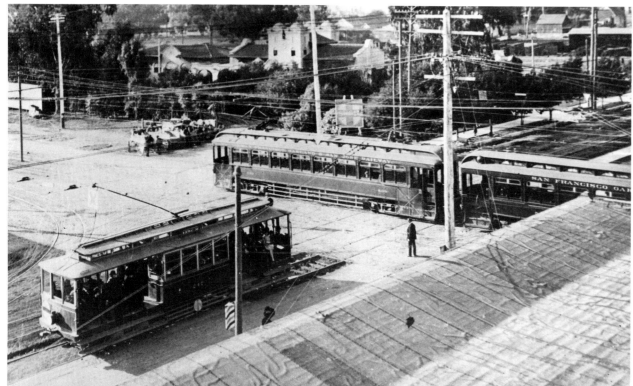

EVEN IN THE FIRST decade of our century, Yerba Buena and San Pablo Ave. was a busy transportation corner. The local streetcar heads north toward Berkeley, while the train of SFO&SJRy 500s carries its passengers to the pier three and one-half miles offshore for the brief marine journey to San Francisco. At top is the Mission style Santa Fe Railway depot. **A.C. Transit**

Growing Longer

AS ADDITIONAL 500 class cars were built to handle growing traffic, their length increased. This was the result of lengthened platforms as well as additional room for seating.

(RIGHT) **THE REALLY LONG** version (69 feet, 3½ inches) is quite a contrast with the 54-foot, 7¼-inch length of the original cars, like No. 501 shown below at left. Cars 517 to 550 were slightly longer than the first batch (58 feet, 5 inches). This car is seen at the Pier in the early days of the system.

Mark Effle Collection

THE FIRST CAR, No. 501, served residents of the Eastshore Empire for almost four decades; the 500s ran until the Bridge Units and the bridge ended their service. These cars seated 68 passengers. No. 501 is shown on a siding along the Key fill in 1936. It was built by the St. Louis Car Company in 1903. **Charles A. Smallwood/Magna Collection**

THE LATER 500s had from 84 to 88 seats (depending on the subgroup) and were some of the longest wooden interurbans ever built. No. 580, seen at 40th and Broadway en route from Piedmont, in March 1936, was built in 1911 by the St. Louis Car Company.

Mark Effle Collection

FRESH OUT OF the paint shop, No. 576 is decorated by not only the Key System Transit Company's new orange (rendered very dark by the film) and cream livery, but two lovely young ladies in the flapper styles of 1927.

E.R. Mohr Collection

Key Trains To The Pier

(BELOW) **A FORMIDABLE TRAIN OF** seven wooden electric coaches, with a 650-class center-door car bring up the rear, fills 40th, near Broadway, in Oakland.　　**A.C. Transit**

(BELOW) **HUNDREDS OF PASSENGERS** were moved expeditiously in long Key trains. Ten 500s stand at Adeline and Alcatraz in South Berkeley (the sign on the pole indicates Southern Pacific's station at that location). Key's electrified system prompted electrification of what had been SP steam-powered suburban train service.

B.H. Ward/E.R. Mohr Collection

THE BEAUTY of this handsome Key train is complemented by the lines of the Hotel Claremont, which was the terminal of what became the "E" transbay route. No. 577 prepares to depart for the Pier in the mid-1930s.

Tom Gray Collection/E.R. Mohr

NORTH TO BERKELEY roars this four-car Key train, seen along the Linden St. right-of-way near Tower Three, where the F and E trains met the C line. Circa 1936.   **Charles A. Smallwood/Magna Collection**

A CLASSIC HEAD-ON view of No. 566 at Yerba Buena yard, near Tower Two. This is one of the 500s built in the Key shops.
Brian Thompson

THIS SUBWAY took the orange trains under the mainline of Southern Pacific to eliminate delays and hazards, since both local "Red Trains" and long-distance passenger and freight traffic gave the SP artery almost constant use. The structure running across the top is a highway access road to the bridge, which opened to auto, bus and truck traffic in 1936. View circa 1937.
Charles A. Smallwood/Magna Collection

13

AS STREAMLINED BRIDGE UNITS began appearing in 1937, they were put into the equipment pool, since they were compatible with the older cars. This made for some interesting sights, as witness this multi-class lashup operating west from San Pablo Ave. along Yerba Buena. The two cars bringing up the rear of this five-car train are 650-class center-door models. **W.C. Whittaker/E.R. Mohr Collection**

Steel Cars For Twelfth Street

THE OAKLAND CITY FATHERS had prohibited operation of Key's giant 500-series trains through downtown Oakland, forcing the company, known then as the San Francisco-Oakland Terminal Railway, to run shuttle cars to 12th and Poplar. The 650s, delivered by the American Car Company in 1918, were designed to look more like streetcars, and were immediately placed into service on the 12th Street line, restoring through service.

(RIGHT) **WITH THE BRIDGE RAILWAY** in mind, Nos. 650 and 652 were made into an articulated train in 1932. The experimental unit is shown at the Pier that year. This "train" became streamlined Bridge Unit No. 100 in the Emeryville Shops in 1937. The bodies and components of other 650s also became part of many of the new Units.

Charles A. Smallwood/Magna Collection

THE LAST CAR of a group constructed by Key System in 1925, No. 688, duplicated the other 650-series cars constructed by the American Car Company in 1918. It is seen here at Lower Yard, next to Tower Two, in Emeryville.

Charles A. Smallwood/Magna Collection

ONE OF THE TWO 650s with railroad-style roofs, No. 664 is pictured along Monterey Blvd. in the northern reaches of Berkeley, in the early 1930s.

L.J. Ciapponi

AS THE BRIDGE nears completion, a train of two 650s and a 500 head toward shore from the Key System pier along the pile trestle.
L.J. Ciapponi

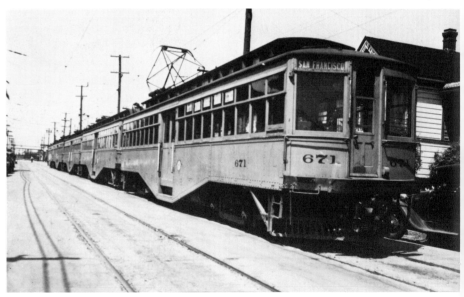

650s IN ACTION: (TOP) No. 683 pauses at the 40th and San Pablo waiting shelter en route to the Pier, in 1936. (ABOVE) Five 650s are photographed along Louise St., at 32nd. In the far distance is the junction with the main line. Circa 1935.
BOTH: Charles A. Smallwood/Magna Collection

(LEFT) **THIS EARLY VIEW** of 650-series trains was taken on 12th Street, the Oakland artery denied to trains of Key's huge 500s.
Randolph Brandt

THIS SPECIAL TRAIN of 650s was sent to Hayward to carry city officials to ceremonies for new Key ferries. This view, taken in San Leandro, shows the use of trolley poles instead of pantographs due to the design of the overhead conductor wire. Some 650s and 500s had poles as well as "pans" for operation over the 22nd Street line.

PASSENGERS TRANSFER to the 500s of the 22nd Street line at Poplar Junction, 22nd and Poplar, during the period through service could not travel into downtown Oakland due to a city ordinance banning the wooden 500-class cars. No. 345 runs in special connecting service from points in Oakland.

Both: Randolph Brandt Collection

THE FERRY TERMINAL for the Richmond-San Rafael Ferry was at
the far north reach of the east bay streetcar system. The car shown at
the terminal of the Richmond car line is No. 272, one of the "Lehighs";
and at far left is a little tower car. The ferry at far right is the CITY OF
SAN RAFAEL.
                                                     Randolph Brandt Collection

Ferryboat Flotilla

ACROSS THE WATERS of San Francisco Bay came the ferries of Key System, giving pre-Bridge commuters two daily voyages. There was much to see, if the fog subsided; ships of the Navy, ocean-going freighters en route to port, railroad car-ferries. This vessel, the TREASURE ISLAND, was built at the Union Iron Works in 1911, as Santa Fe Railway's SAN PEDRO. It came to Key System in 1938 and its new name was appropriate to its service, carrying Exposition construction workers and employees to that fabled island. The boat served as a floating barracks during World War II. In this view, TREASURE ISLAND approaches the San Francisco Ferry Building from the Exposition, June 1940.   Warren K. Miller

(ABOVE) **THE CLAREMONT** was built in Alameda in 1907 and later became the GOLDEN WAY of Southern Pacific-Golden Gate Ferries.

(ABOVE) **THE SAN FRANCISCO** was constructed in 1905 by James W. Dickie & Sons, Alameda. It later ran as the GOLDEN DAWN of Southern Pacific-Golden Gate Ferries and ended its days as a fish reduction plant.

(RIGHT) **BUILT BY THE** Los Angeles Shipbuilding & Dry Dock Corp. of San Pedro, Calif., the HAYWARD entered service in 1923. It moved around after Key's ferry service was discontinued, being sent first to Portland, Oregon, for service to shipyards for the U.S. Maritime Commission in 1943. It steamed south to Astoria, Oregon, later that year then was towed to San Francisco where it continued to haul workers to San Francisco bay shipyards. Following its yeoman wartime service it was sold for scrap in 1947.

Steaming To The City
On The San Leandro

THE KEELS OF this boat and the HAYWARD were laid June 28, 1922, at Los Angeles Shipbuilding & Dry Dock Corp. in San Pedro, Calif. After the outbreak of World War II it joined the Hayward in shipyard service (see page 20). The SAN LEANDRO was snapped from a passing ferry in June 1940 on the way from the Golden Gate Exposition to San Francisco; the skyline was then devoid of pointed buildings and 40-plus story skyscrapers. (Mottling is due to deterioration of the negative.)

Warren K. Miller

San Francisco Approach

THE YERBA BUENA shown in this 1940 view as it steams from San Francisco to the Exposition was the second ferry to bear that name, the first being a vessel launched from the Dickie yard in Alameda in 1903. This boat was delivered to Key in 1927 and after closure of ferry service it joined many other Key ferries in wartime shipyard service. For a time after April 1945 it carried troops between San Francisco, Oakland and Pittsburg.

THE TOWER of San Francisco's famed Ferry Building crowns the terminal as we see the slips from waterside. At left is Southern Pacific's ALAMEDA, then the forms of Key System's TREASURE ISLAND and YERBA BUENA. From the first building behind the tower, Southern Pacific executives could view their "navy" at work. Photo taken in August 1940.   **Both: Warren K. Miller**

(FACING PAGE) **THE WEST'S MOST FAMOUS** landmark, the San Francisco Ferry Building sits astride the foot of Market Street. This view of the mid-1920s shows Market Street Railway's "White Front" streetcars looping in front of the terminal (and two Municipal Railway trolleys at center and far right). The large vessel at left is the DELTA QUEEN, just in from its Sacramento River run. The double-deck Embarcadero freeway now covers the foreground.

Southern Pacific

Key Route Pier

MILLIONS OF BOARD FEET of lumber went into construction of the great Key pier and attendant trestle. Francis Marion "Borax" Smith's Key Route brought great improvements to transbay passengers, since its new electric train and ferryboat service was much faster than Southern Pacific steam-powered trains and longer ferry journey.

(ABOVE) **THIS EARLY VIEW** shows the fill and trestle (left) which replaced the original, all-trestle alignment. As originally built, from the middle of the boat slip to the west end of the subway under the Southern Pacific tracks at the water's edge, it was 16,240 feet long, an engineering marvel of its time.

A.C. Transit

(LEFT) **FROM THE AIR,** the trestle and pier are very impressive. In this later photo, the original route has been removed except for a short stub at the pier end, used for car storage. The shoreline has crept westward in the following decades.

Robert A. Burrowes Collection

(FACING PAGE) **THE BOAT SLIPS** and the impressive, medieval style terminal and trainshed are captured in this early aerial view. The YERBA BUENA steams out of its slip while the FERNWOOD and the CLAREMONT lay over.

Robert A. Burrowes Collection

(ABOVE) **THE FAMOUS** "Key Route" emblem is emblazoned on the Pier's trainshed, which bears the road's full corporate title. Locomotive No. 1001 awaits a call to duty at right. This view was taken in October 1919 during a strike, when all cars carried large banners reading "The Cars of This Company Are Operated Under An Injunction of the Federal Court."

Robert A. Burrowes

(FACING PAGE) **THIS SPECTACLE** of electric trains greeted patrons as they disembarked at the Key Route Pier. The two cars behind No. 582, at right, are 650-series center-door types.

Randolph Brandt Collection

(ABOVE) **LOOK CLOSELY** at this interior view of the Pier, directly behind the train location sign, and you'll see the experimental articulated train, No. 650, built in 1932, a precursor of the later bridge units.
A.C. Transit

(BELOW) **CONSTRUCTION OF** the new bridge proceeds in this mid-1930s view of the Pier. The newer building at its end is the replacement for the original terminal destroyed in a disastrous blaze on May 6, 1933. A power failure prevented fire-fighting equipment from being rushed to the Pier (see also P. 110), so 14 cars and the ferry PERALTA were lost (the hulk of the Peralta, sold to a salvage dealer, was somehow rebuilt and saw further service on the Black Ball line in Puget Sound as the KALAKALA). The new terminal was opened in October 1934.
A.C. Transit

THE NEW BRIDGE is open, but the trestle and pier remain in this late 1930s picture postcard view, which is included to show the relative positions of the two structures. The back side of the card remarks, "....this stupendous bridge (built at a cost of $77,000,000)." **Magna Collection**

BACK WHEN ARCHES gave directions instead of signifying a hamburger emporium, Berkeley erected this fine structure at University and San Pablo. "Lehigh" streetcar No. 280 heads south from Richmond.

THE KEY ROUTE INN, an architectural gem at 22nd and Broadway in Oakland, was only one of "Borax" Smith's non-railway projects. He also built the Claremont Hotel at the end of the 55th St. (later E) line, developed Piedmont Park for the 40th St. (later C) line, and created Idora Park, in North Oakland. The emblem superimposed at top right is from a 1906 magazine advertisement for the hostelry.

Randolph Brandt Collection

(FACING PAGE) **A LONG STRING** of 500s poses for the photographer at the back side of the Key Route Inn, in October 1915. The arch area, spanning 22nd Street provided a covered terminal. All the mufti-clad "brass" seem to be smoking cigars while the nattily attired crew abstain from the habit, per the rule book's prohibition.

Randolph Brandt Collection

31

THE ELMHURST CAR HOUSE, located on East 14th Street at 96th Avenue.   **Randolph Brandt Collection**

Piedmont-Bound

HEADING TOWARD its Piedmont terminal at Oakland Avenue, this C line Unit has just left the junction with the No. 10 local streetcar line, with which the transbay line shared trackage from 41st and Piedmont Ave. The No. 10 line continued on the upper level at right.

Robert T. McVay

DOWNTOWN OAKLAND as seen in the early 20s in this view at 14th, San Pablo (at angle) and Broadway (tracks crossing in foreground). Oakland's attractive City Hall is at left. The "C" line was a local car route (Grand Ave.-Hollis). **E.R. Mohr Collection**

(FACING PAGE) **LOOKING DOWN TELEGRAPH AVENUE** toward Broadway, in downtown Oakland, circa 1939. No. 360 is still in East Bay Street Railway's turquoise and cream while the 900-class trolley in the distance bears the newer East Bay Transit Company colors. A "curb census" shows a predomination of Fords, but isn't that a "bathtub" Hudson at far right? **A.C. Transit**

THE C LINE terminal was right at Oakland Avenue's sidewalk. Latham St. is at right.
Robert T. McVay

(UPPER LEFT) **THE FINAL KEY SYSTEM** colors, the so-called "fruit salad" scheme of National City Lines, are still fresh in this August 1947 portrait of Unit No. 124, one of the narrow-window, straight side cars. It's heading west at Yerba Buena and San Pablo, as a local car travels north on San Pablo toward Ashby. **Robert T. McVay**

(LEFT) **THE TRAINSHED** of the 41st and Piedmont terminal frames No. 165, en route to San Francisco, in August 1946.
A.R. Alter

SOUTHERN PACIFIC displays its new "Shasta Daylight" equipment on the former IER tracks at South Berkeley, in 1949. "Straight-side" Unit No. 116 passes en route to downtown Berkeley.   **Brian Thompson**

(FACING PAGE) **EAST BAY TERMINAL,** the bridge railway's San Francisco terminal, at 1st and Mission was mobbed on January 14, 1939, for the dedication of the transbay rail line.

Robert S. Ford Collection

ALIGHTING AT A safety island along Broadway, a shopper leaves No. 942 before it proceeds to Piedmont. Perhaps the lady is planning some purchases at Capwells (at right). Circa mid-1930s.
A.C. Transit

(UPPER LEFT) **WESTBOUND** on 22nd St., No. 136 crosses the intersection of Adeline St., on its B line journey to the bridge. The spur inside the framework of the building at left is electrified for Key freight service. Photo taken July 1955.
Jim Walker

(ABOVE) **TOWARD THE END** of streetcar service, in 1947, No. 816 operates west on University Avenue at Shattuck, downtown Berkeley. Behind is the campus of the University of California.
Robert T. McVay

(LEFT) No. 7 car 963 runs by the fountain at the great circle, Arlington and Marin, Berkeley, near the Thousand Oaks Tunnel, in August 1946.
A.R. Alter

(RIGHT) **THE "CITY OF BERKELEY"** train, five former Sacramento Northern interurban cars retained after that road ceased operation over the bridge, pulls into the East Bay Terminal in August 1947.

(BELOW) **BRIDGE UNIT** No. 167 operates on the Shattuck Avenue portion of the F line that utilized the former Southern Pacific Berkeley line after its closure in 1941. No. 167 is preserved at the Orange Empire Railway Museum, Perris, Calif. (Nos. 182 and 186 are displayed at the California Railway Museum, Rio Vista Junction, Calif.).

(BELOW, RIGHT) **THE ONLY SURVIVING** "Lehigh" streetcar, No. 271, was purchased by the Bay Area Electric Railroad Assn. and ran on many excursions, like this November 21, 1948, jaunt, marking the end of the last streetcar lines. No. 271 is viewed on Shattuck Ave., near Addison, in Berkeley.

All views this page: Robert T. McVay

SMALLER WINDOWS, STRAIGHT SIDES characteriz
bridge units Nos. 100-124. This body style was being cc
structed at the same time as the slope side-type and we
within one quarter inch of their width. No. 113 is in B line se
vice on Lakeshore Ave. at MacArthur Blvd., in 1956.

Harry W. Demo

LARGE WINDOW, SLOPE SIDE variety of the articulated units built for the bridge railway is illustrated by this November 1946 view of No. 133 along the main line next to Emeryville Shops. Nos. 125 to 187 were built in this configuration. Although No. 133 has just been painted in National City Lines' yellow on its lower half, and green around the windows, the silver roof (including the "Key System" lettering) has been retained.

Brian Thompson

(LEFT) **ROLLING ALONG** the 11 line private right-of-way, No. 716 is captured on film in March 1948.

(LEFT, BELOW) No. 948 shows its new Key System Transit Lines colors in August 1947 as it rolls through downtown Oakland on the No. 1 line. Note the sealed rear door, part of the one-man operation modifications of the early 1930s.

(BELOW) **PAUSING FOR A PHOTOGRAPH** on a September 21, 1947, railfan excursion, No. 355 is seen on the No. 14 line.

All views this page: Robert T. McVay

(RIGHT) **ONLY SIX MONTHS** remain for streetcar service in the East Bay as No. 966 operates on the No. 11 line, in May 1948.

(BELOW) **UNDER THE CATENARY** of the F transbay line, No. 967 turns back on the No. 4 line, at Shattuck and University, downtown Berkeley, in August 1947.

(BELOW, RIGHT) No. 953 passes the Grand Lake Theatre, on Grand Ave., Oakland, in May 1948, before television had cut into movie and popcorn sales. **All views this page: Robert T. McVay**

Home-Built Bridge Units

EMERYVILLE SHOPS proved its mettle once again when the bridge railway's equipment needs were determined by turning out Units Nos. 100-104. (The others were built by Bethlehem Steel and the St. Louis Car Co.) (RIGHT) In this 1937 view the frames of 650 class are going through the "metamorphosis." Many of the units utilized structural, electrical or furnishing components from the 500 and 650 classes.
Charles A. Smallwood/Magna Collection

"HOMEMADE" UNIT No. 101 poses at the Bridge Yard as a three-car train of IER's red cars speed by on new flyover viaduct, circa 1941.
Mark Effle Collection

INSIDE AN ARTICULATED bridge unit was found 124 seats, plus room for many dozens more rush-hour standees. (ABOVE, LEFT) The conductor rests at a line terminal in the non-smoking (B) section. (ABOVE, RIGHT) A view from the other shows the smoking (A) section (most had rattan seats; these have been covered with upholstery).

Jim Walker

(LEFT) **THE ARTICULATION** was covered with a metal guard to keep pedestrians from attempting daredevil stunts. The portal between sections was kept weather-tight with a metal and fabric diaphragm. The device above the first window to the left of the portal was a trip arm to raise the pantograph as trains left the third-rail electrification on the bridge. This center truck of the units was not motorized (for their size, their four motors made them underpowered).

Interurbans

(BELOW) **ONE HUNDRED FEET,** five and one-half inches of crowd-carrying capacity. No. 102 is seen at Bridge Yard alongside the toll plaza in 1947.

Brian Thompson

THIS "F" TRAIN of bridge units exits the south portal of the Northbrae Tunnel, in the northern reaches of Berkeley, in 1946.

A.R. Alter

Bridge Scenes

(ABOVE, LEFT) **A RUSH HOUR** F line three-unit set, headed by N 154, travels the bridge railway eastbound toward Berkeley in the sur mer of 1956. Most auto traffic ran on the upper deck, in both dire tions, while trucks, buses and a few autos ran on three lanes on th lower level (the middle lane was reservable, using signals, for t predominate flow of traffic).

Jim Walk

(ABOVE) **A LATE AFTERNOON "A" TRAIN** leaves East Bay Te minal in 1956. The overhead wire seen here is a vestige of the IER ar Sacramento Northern operations. The trolley wire system on t bridge was removed during the war for reuse on the Richmo Shipyard Railway, since the Key trains used third-rail curre collection.

G.C. Whi

(LEFT) **EN ROUTE** to Eastbay Terminal, this 3-unit train is on one lo of the loop, as we look back along the Bay Bridge to Yerba Bue Island (distance). A few feet further it will loop 180 degrees to enter t terminal building. View circa 1956.

Jim Walk

East Bay Terminal

TAKING LEAVE OF San Francisco, the passengers on Unit No. 158 head toward Oakland on the B line. The six-track terminal was opened in January 1939 and was served by many San Francisco Municipal Railway streetcar lines. **G.C. White/Magna Collection**

(BELOW, LEFT) **LATE EVENING MOOD:** A Key Unit looms from one of the terminal ramps. **Magna Collection**

(BELOW) **UNIT NO. 169** has just closed its doors and awaits clearance to leave the terminal for its bay crossing to Oakland points in this October 1957 view. **Allan W. Styffe**

51

(ABOVE) **BEHIND** "A" Unit No. 155, running in third-rail territory east of the Bay Bridge can be seen the two parts of the impressive span and the San Francisco skyline.   Denzel C. Allen, Jr.

52

(BELOW) A three-unit E train approaches the end of third-rail at Bridge Yard in an evening rush-hour in 1956.

Jim Walker

Bridge Yard Scenes

(RIGHT) **IT'S MIDAFTERNOON** as a single-unit F train No. 136 pauses at Bridge Yard en route to San Francisco, circa 1955. The yard is adjacent to the toll plaza area. Both the roadway and the yard were expansions of the fill that formerly led to the Key pier.   **Harre W. Demoro**

(BELOW) **ON A GRAY DAY** in June 1956, B train No. 180 leaves the Bridge Yard stop. Note the unit is still propelled by electricity in the third rail. A few feet further a trackside trip device will activate the "whisker" on the unit's roof, which in turn will cause the pantograph to raise to the catenary, which begins at this point.   **Jim Walker**

(BELOW, RIGHT) **ELBOW POWER** is applied to the picture windows of unit No. 163 at Bridge Yard near Key System's shop building, in 1940.   **Mark Effle Collection**

Bridge Railway Shops

KEY UNITS AWAIT SERVICING in the Bridge Yard shops in the early 1950s—part of the extensive complex built for the new railway across the San Francisco Bay span.
(RIGHT) Denzel C. Allen, Jr.
(BELOW) Jim Walker

54

Taking the A Train

AT THE JUNCTION of the A and B trains with the main line, west of Emeryville Shops, a midafternoon "A" train passes Tower Two on its way toward downtown Oakland. The track crossing in the foreground goes from the Shops to the Lower Yard. View taken in October 1943.   **Brian Thompson**

(RIGHT) **THE BIG CURVE** at 12th and Poplar St. is filled with an A line wartime shipyard tripper, which will run to the junction (shown in photo above) at Tower Two where homeward-bound workers from the Richmond Shipyard will transfer from trains serving the wartime electric railway, then head to Havenscourt terminal. The date: July 1943.   **Brian Thompson**

Key Equipment Preserved

FORTUNATELY not all of the Key System is a memory, thanks to the efforts of aficionados of the Key System. You can still see and ride Key System rolling stock at the California Railway Museum, Rio Vista Junction (on Cal. Hwy. 12 about 10 miles east of Fairfield). The Key collection includes streetcars 271 and 987, bridge units 182 and 186, shipyard railway cars 561 and 563, locomotive 1001, wrecker 1011, line car 1201, shop switcher 1215 and line car 1218. Bridge unit 167 is occasionally operated at the Orange Empire Railway Museum, Perris, Calif. (17 miles south of Riverside on Interstate 15-E).

A Line Extensions

WHEN RED TRAINS ceased operation on IER's 7th St. line along Bancroft to Dutton Ave., in San Leandro on March 21, 1941, Key System concurrently extended its "A" trains out its 14th St. local line to 105th Ave. (ABOVE) Passengers have just disembarked from a two-unit train at that temporary terminal. By April 14 of that year, "A" trains had been rerouted along a portion of the ex-IER line (RIGHT) to a terminal at Havenscourt Blvd., three miles short of the old IER line end.

TOP: **L.J. Ciapponi/Roger Ciapponi Collection**
RIGHT: **Magna Collection**

12th & Broadway

ONE SUNNY AFTERNOON in downtown Oakland, Unit No. 122 heads a two-unit "A" train on 12th Street bound for San Francisco. The cross street is important Broadway, and the yellow, green and white colors on the White bus at extreme right tells us this is soon after the sale of Key System to National City Lines. **Magna Collection**

(BELOW, LEFT) **12th STREET,** downtown Oakland resounds with the rumble of another Key "A" train in the early 1950s. (BELOW) Looking west along 12th Street, Unit No. 156 and second unit dominate the pavement. Both photos were taken at Broadway.
Magna Collection

57

(BELOW) **THE UNDERHILLS TERMINAL** of the B line was a sylvan spot amid attractive residences. We look toward end of track as No. 186 awaits its passengers for a return trip to Oakland and San Francisco, in 1956. The upper destination blind is being rolled and at the snap of **the shutter,** shows a former terminal of the A line.   **Jim Walker**

Trestle Glen

ALONG THE CURVED right-of-way bowles Unit No. 112 near the B line's Underhills terminal, circa 1956. Service began on this extension from 22nd & Broadway in 1921.   **G.L. White**

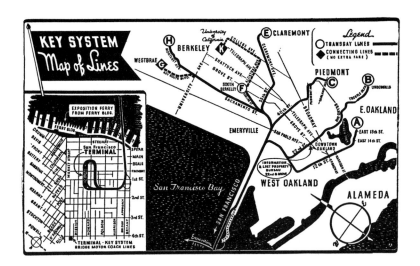

NEAR THE OUTER END of the "C" line, Unit No. 131 takes its afternoon run to San Francisco in the mid-1950s.   Denzel C. Allen, Jr.

C Line Station

(LEFT) **THIS HAND-SOME** structure provided a deluxe station for Key System C line trains at 41st St. & Piedmont Ave., in Oakland. We look toward Oakland, as a No. 10 car proceeds down Piedmont Ave in this 1939 view.
Magna Collection

(BELOW, LEFT) **A WORK CAR** train headed by Differential dump No. 1276 brings material to the site during construction of the Piedmont Ave. station, in 1937. At this time, the outer end of the "C" line ran as a shuttle, served in this view by No. 956, equipped with pantograph and pilot.
Charles A. Smallwood/ Magna Collection

(BELOW) **IN THIS** 1940 view of the station's trainshed, outer-end "C" line shuttle No. 956 awaits transfer passengers. One of the bridge units sits inside the shed on a third, stub track. Buses also met trains at this facility.
C.E. Wright/Mark Effle Collection

EXCLUSIVE PIEDMONT was served by the outer end of the C transbay line. (ABOVE) Unit No. 131 prepares to leave the Latham St. and Oakland Ave. terminal, in the early 1950s. **Denzel C. Allen, Jr.** (RIGHT) This right-of-way, with its wandering track alignment, gave departing units from the Oakland Ave. terminal a rollercoaster style downhill start on their way to San Francisco. **Jim Walker** (BELOW) The terminal had a handsome, tile-roofed waiting station. Shuttle car No. 955 awaits return passengers in March 1940, for its trip to 41st and Piedmont Ave. transfer station. **Mark Effle Collection**

GUESTS OF THE POSH Claremont Hotel had a truly direct rail connection to Bay Area points, and while they played tennis they could watch departing and arriving E trains at this, probably the most novel terminal on the Key System, between tennis courts on the hotel grounds! **Denzel C. Allen, Jr.**

DOWN A GARDEN PATH . . . an electric train! The E line terminal is seen from the hotel grounds of the Claremont. **Jim Walker**

Shattuck Views

THESE TWO VIEWS of downtown Berkeley look north, at Allston Way. (ABOVE) This photo, taken in the late 1940s, show both routes used by Key's Berkeley trains over the decades. At left is the former IER line, which the Orange and Silver Trains used following the demise of the Red Trains in 1941 (the stub track in the center was used by IER's electric mail car). To the right is the track originally used by the Key Route cars, which terminated at University Ave. and at this time still used by Key's local streetcars.　　**Magna Collection**

(RIGHT) A bit later, a photographer shot this panorama from the Shattuck Hotel, and caught a two-unit F train headed south toward Oakland. At this point BART now serves Berkeley underground.　　**Magna Collection**

Electric Railway Panorama

A SIX TRACK SPECTACLE along Adeline St. in South Berkeley, at the Alcatraz Ave. station. In this mid-1930s panorama at left, East Bay Transit's No. 3 line ran a short distance along Adeline while going between two cross streets. For the S.P. Red Trains (center) this was but a way stop en route to Thousand Oaks, but for Key's F trains, this was end-of-line.

Tom Gray Collection/E.R. Mohr

(RIGHT) **THE KEY SYSTEM'S F** trains ran on parallel tracks with Southern Pacific "big red trains" along Shattuck Avenue and Adeline Avenue. The 3-unit Key train is at the F line's Alcatraz Avenue terminal while the IER train has come south from downtown Berkeley.   E.R. Mohr

(BELOW) **A LATER A.M. VIEW,** rush-hour traffic past, shows a single IER "3" route car stopped at its South Berkeley station as a single-unit Key F train sits at its Berkeley terminal station, designated as "Alcatraz & Adeline St. Station." Such two-railway scenes with the new Key System cars lasted only until the Southern Pacific abandoned its suburban electric network in 1941. At left of the "big red train" can be seen the overhead of East Bay Transit's No. 3 streetcar line which made this a six-track railway for a few blocks!

L.J. Ciapponi/Roger Ciapponi Collection

Football Extra

LAYING OVER NORTH OF DOWNTOWN BERKELEY, unit No. 122 bears white flags indicating it is an extra train, in this instance a football extra serving a big game at the University of California. It waits for the contest to end on a Fall afternoon in the early 1950s.

Denzel C. Allen, Jr.

Berryman

THE F LINE TRACKAGE around the Berryman stop was a favorite with photographers, who trekked north of downtown Berkeley over the years. Until 1941, Southern Pacific's "Red Trains" ran along here on the Shattuck Ave. line. The light was best in the afternoon, when (RIGHT) a three-unit F train heads toward Thousand Oaks in the 1940s. **Brian Thompson** (BELOW) In the early 1950s, three straight-sided Units traverse the same area. Note the lead unit has a tan roof while the second and third are still in white. All active units were painted tan on top by 1958. **Denzel C. Allen, Jr.** (BELOW, RIGHT) Looking the other way, toward Northbrae, we see a four-unit train taking a crossover. **Mark Effle Collection**

Former Red Train Territory

THE THOUSAND OAKS terminal of the F line, at Solano Ave. and The Alameda, was formerly a part of the loop formed by Southern Pacific's Ninth St. and Shattuck Ave. electric lines. Following the IER abandonment in 1941, Key ran only to Northbrae, but resumed service through the Northbrae tunnel to The Alameda in December 1942.

(ABOVE) **A THREE-UNIT** F train waits at the north portal of the Northbrae tunnel for space at the single-track terminal (shown below). After the abandonment of rail service in 1958, a street was opened through the bore.   Denzel C. Allen, Jr.

(RIGHT) **THE TERMINAL** of the F line on a Summer day in 1956.   Jim Walker

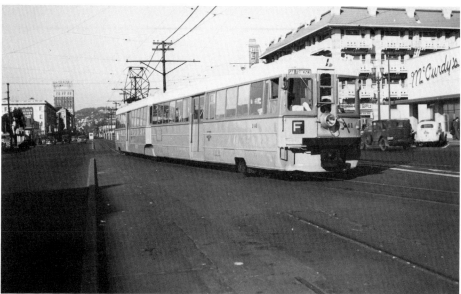

ALTHOUGH KEY's BERKELEY LINE (later called the F line) was its first, in 1903, it was cut back along the parallel S.P. electric line to Alcatraz Ave. in 1933. So, when the Red Trains were up for abandonment, permission was contingent on extension of the F line to downtown Berkeley. To accomplish this a single-track was placed into service along the old alignment to Ward St., where a connection was made with the East Bay Transit No. 4 streetcar line on Shattuck Ave. to the east side of the square, at University Ave. Berkeley authorized extension of Key rail service to the south portal of Northbrae tunnel, and to accomplish this (ABOVE) the line along Shattuck was curved onto the former SP/IER tracks at Dwight Way.
Magna Collection; E.R. Mohr

BY 1956, TRACK MAINTENANCE was best described as "deferred." This view, looking north along Adeline St. at Market St. shows how broken the pavement had become adjacent to the rails. Wide holes at each rail joint were the result of years of pounding without tightening and raising.
Jim Walker

Trains to the Shipyard

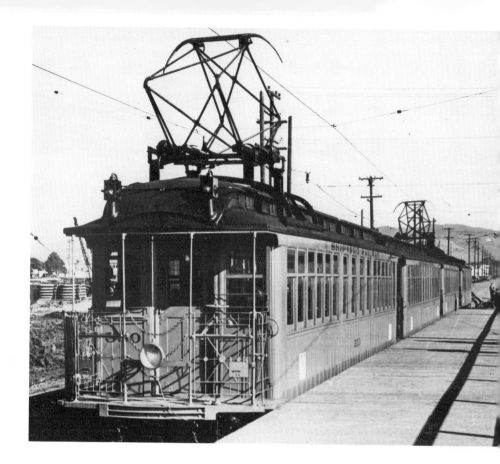

AWAITING HOMEWARD SHIPYARD WORKERS, a four-car train of ex-New York elevated cars is seen at the Richmond Shipyard loading platform during the World War II year of 1943. This vital transport artery was assembled using these second-hand cars, rails and overhead from abandoned electric lines and rights-of-way created from various rail and road routes. **A.C. Transit**

NEWLY ARRIVED FROM NEW YORK, two of the former I.R.T. elevated cars (BELOW) await modifications. They emerged with new paint jobs (BELOW, RIGHT) and minor changes, such as headlight location. No. 557 was one of two Shipyard Railway cars with wooden pilots (salvaged from Key System cars).

Left: **Magna Collection,**
Right: **Mark Effle Collection**

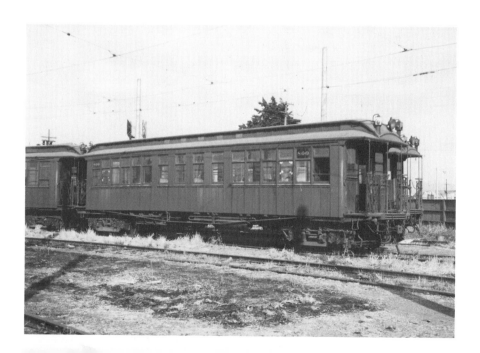

EN ROUTE to the high-level platforms at 40th & Yerba Buena, No. 565 brings up the rear of a Richmond Shipyard-bound train. It runs on a third track alongside the Key System main line—first stop was a platform at the junction of the main and the A and B lines. At left is a portion of the Santa Fe Railway depot. **Mark Effle Collection**

TWO TRAINING TRAINS pause for photographs at the Gilman crossing in Berkeley prior to the advent of regular service on the Shipyard Railway. **Dick Jenevein/Mark Effle Collection**

AS OLD AS THEY WERE (almost all were built before 1890), the New York cars looked impressive on film, a freshly painted part of our war effort in this view, circa 1943. **Mark Effle Collection**

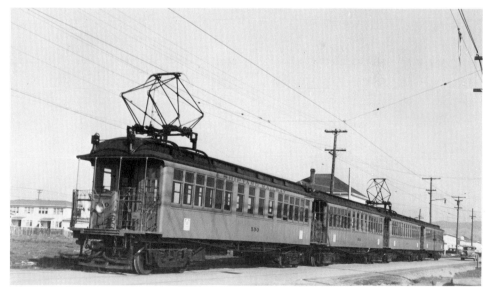

THIS FOUR-CAR train, headed by No. 550, was snapped on Potrero Avenue, Richmond, in February 1943. The metal pilots were salvaged from the Interurban Electric Railway "red cars." **Mark Effle Collection**

Rails to Richmond, in Record Time

(LEFT) **RACING ALONG** Hoffman Blvd. on the Shipyard Railway, bridge unit No. 134 heads toward the 40th & San Pablo terminal. Some of the overhead and rail for the emergency service came from Key's late "H" line, and other trolley wire came from the overhead on the bridge railway, no longer needed since demise of the IER Big Red Trains. Key trains used third rail on the bridge. **Brian Thompson**

(BELOW, LEFT) **UNIT NO. 177** heads a two-unit train toward Richmond along the future alignment of 9th St., north of Harrison, at the Berkeley-Albany border. (BELOW, RIGHT) Turning to the opposite direction, the photographer caught a Bridge Unit descending the trestle built to carry shipyard trains over the Southern Pacific main line. **Both: Brian Thompson**

(RIGHT) A BREAK IN THE CROSS-WALK lines indicates the newly laid tracks along San Pablo Ave. for Richmond Shipyard Railway use. This stretch was formerly the streetcar line to Richmond, abandoned in 1933 beyond Ashby Ave. No. 174 heads south, passing the H.J. Heinz factory, in 1944.   **Brian Thompson**

(BELOW) WORLD WAR II was 14 months old on January 31, 1943, when this view was taken at the Ashby and San Pablo Ave. terminal of the No. 2 streetcar line. Gas rationing was coming into force and all buses from Richmond now terminated here to transfer passengers to the streetcar for downtown Oakland. The four-car shipyard train is on its way to Richmond, about to meet a 1939 Key CM Mack (far left). In the terminal streetcar No. 823 waits to pull out onto San Pablo.
                Warren K. Miller

(BELOW, RIGHT) A UNIT CROSSES its normal path. No. 134 crosses the main line at 40th & San Pablo, after which it will turn into the special Shipyard Railway platform on the west side of the street. Note wartime dimmer cap on the streetlight at right.
                Brian Thompson

PASSING BY SUBSTATION No. 2 of the Richmond Shipyard Railway, Unit. No. 185 heads south at Buchanan St., in Albany, on an afternoon in April 1943. **Mark Effle Collection**

CURVING AWAY from the parallel Southern Pacific mainline, a brace of six former elevated cars winds its way along Hoffman Blvd. in Richmond toward the shipyards. The light-colored building behind the fourth and fifth cars is one of the line's substations. **Interurbans**

Exposition Trains

ALTHOUGH DIRECT RAIL SERVICE to San Francisco via the Bridge Railway was inaugurated January 15, 1939, train-ferry service remained to carry the throngs attending the 1939 season of the Golden Gate Exposition on Treasure Island.　　　**Interurbans**

(RIGHT) **BACK FROM THE PIER,** a two-car X train approaches the San Pablo crossing, in June 1939. (Note that the two views on this page, as well as others, render the orange lower portion of the Units rather dark, a phenomenon of the orthochromatic film used by many photographers in the period.)
Mark Effle Collection

(BELOW) **BEARING A SPECIAL "X"** designation, a Pier-bound exposition train speeds along the Yerba Buena right-of-way next to Emeryville Shops (to the right) in June 1939. "X" trains ran on all the transbay lines.
Mark Effle Collection

A CASUALTY OF CAR SHORTAGES, the H line was the "other" transbay line. Routes A-B-C-E-F ran until the end of all rail service, but Key's Sacramento St. route was abandoned in 1941 because there were not enough railcars to go around when Key System took over portions of Southern Pacific's electric system. Unit No. 169 pauses at Sacramento and University, Berkeley. Behind is a railfan excursion car and bringing up the rear is G line shuttle car 955 or 956.

Mark Effle Collection

H Line

(ABOVE) **READY FOR A CHANGE** at University Ave., G (Westbrae) shuttle car No. 956 poses next to H Unit No. 169 north of the intersection not long before the demise of both lines in July 1941. **Warren K. Miller**

(LEFT) **OUTBOUND H PASSEN-GERS** pass Tower Three, just east of Yerba Buena & San Pablo, aboard Unit No. 111 in June 1941. It will share the F line's two tracks on a four-track right-of-way for a short distance, then veer to the left to Sacramento St.

Warren K. Miller

A SECOND CAREER was in store for five former Sacramento Northern interurban cars as a result of the World War II traffic surge. Stored after that company's 1941 abandonment of passenger service into San Francisco, ownership had been vested in the Toll Bridge Authority. Key System, in dire need of additional seats for its passengers, purchased the cars, then made minor modifications, such as adding seats in former baggage compartments, and installation of markers and destination roller signs.

(RIGHT) **THE FIVE CAR** train was assigned to the F line, and its daily rush-hour trip became known to many as the "City of Berkeley." Here detraining passengers walk toward Solano Ave. at the Thousand Oaks terminal. Note that all the men are wearing suits, vests and hats in this August 1943 view. **Mark Effle Collection**

"City of Berkeley"

BERKELEY-BOUND, the ex-Sacramento Northern cars cross 40th St. in Emeryville, just after leaving the junction at Tower Three in 1943. **Charles Savage/Mark Effle Collection**

NO LONGER RUNNING to Sacramento and Chico on the Sacramento Northern interurban railway, the five cars purchased by Key System continue their transportation labors in this June 1943 view, approaching the San Francisco terminal. A Bay Bridge tower is in the right background. **Mark Effle Collection**

NOW BEARING the "fruit salad" (yellow, green and white) scheme of the final years of the Key System rail operations, the ex-SN train returns to the storage yard for the night after its evening run to Thousand Oaks, passing Dwight Way on Shattuck Ave., Berkeley.
Addison H. Laflin, Jr./Magna Collection

ON EX-IER TRACK, the five-car "City of Berkeley" heads inbound from Thousand Oaks, at Virginia station, in May 1949.
Addison H. Laflin, Jr./Magna Collection

TAKING THE CURVE at Shattuck and Rose north of downtown Berkeley, the ex-S.N. train rumbles under the catenary of the outer end of the F line. **Warren K. Miller**

BRANCHING OFF THE H line just north of University Ave. in Berkeley, the G-Westbrae shuttle ran to the Albany city line. Two 900-series streetcars were modified for this Key division private-right-of-way route by addition of pilots, and a change from trolley pole to pantograph collectors. The other railroad in this November 1940 view is the Santa Fe's main line into Oakland, which the G line paralleled for much of its length (a shade over two miles). Grand plans to build along this alignment in a proposed "Key Route Blvd." into El Cerrito and Richmond never came to pass, but the BART Richmond line nearly duplicated the G line alignment. **Warren K. Miller**

GRADE CROSSINGS were numerous on the Westbrae line. "Santa Fe" on the crossing sign refers to that railroad's main line, behind the camera. Gilman station is in the left background. View was taken November 1940. **Warren K. Miller**

THE OPEN SPACES are gone (but so is the G line, abandoned in 1941). The right-of-way at right leads to the line's junction with the H line, just north of Sacramento St. and University Ave. **Warren K. Miller**

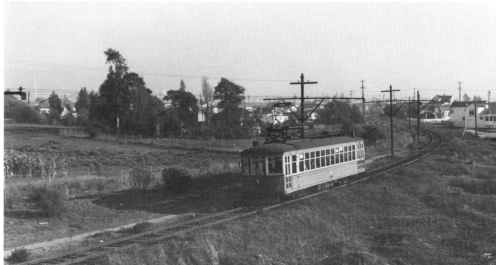

Westbrae Shuttle

(RIGHT) **THE PANTOGRAPH** collector and pilot gave No. 956 (and sister car 955), an interurban flavor in this Westbrae line assignment. Note the catenary support poles for two tracks; one sufficed for this shuttle service.

Mark Effle Collection

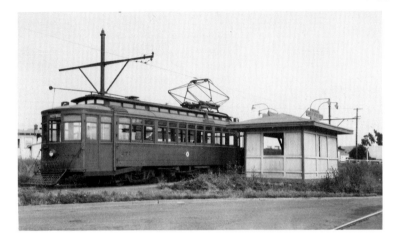

"LEHIGH" streetcar No. 271 was the spare Westbrae shuttle car. (ABOVE) It is seen at the Santa Fe Ave. (Westbrae) terminal of the G line in 1941. **Mark Effle Collection** (BELOW) A handsome portrait of No. 271 outside of Emeryville Shops. **Brian Thompson**

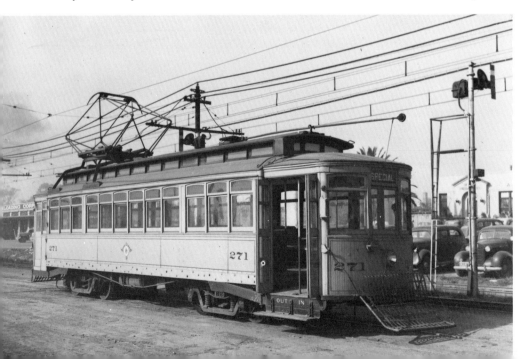

(RIGHT) **ON FOOTBALL DAYS** the K line did not reverse on Bancroft but continued south on Telegraph to make a loop and return to Adeline and Alcatraz for more passengers transferring from the F line. No. 980 and second car make the turn from Telegraph onto Alcatraz on a November Saturday in 1940.   **Warren K. Miller**

(BELOW) **NEARING THE ADELINE TERMINAL,** Nos. 987 and 988 are on Alcatraz Ave. and Dover St. performing Golden Gate Exposition connecting service in 1939.
     Ken Kidder/E.R. Mohr Collection

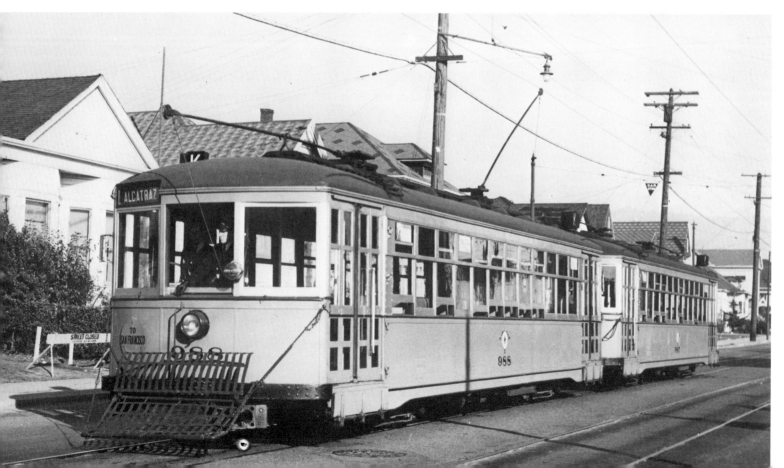

Alcatraz Connection

MULTIPLE UNIT streetcars were a fixture on the K-College Ave. line, which went through many other designations (L, 31 and G) and was abandoned in 1946. The K connected with the through Berkeley trains at Adeline St. and Alcatraz Ave., ran along the latter to College Ave., then north to Bancroft Way and back to Telegraph Ave. No. 982 and train carry a boisterous load of "Old Blues" (or "Reds") heading for the University of California's Memorial Stadium on Big Game Day, 1940.   **Warren K. Miller**

(FACING PAGE) **A TEST TRAIN** composed of No. 117 and second unit sits on Track 6 of East Bay Terminal in San Francisco on January 6, 1939, nine days before revenue service was inaugurated.

Jack Gutte/Robert S. Ford Collection

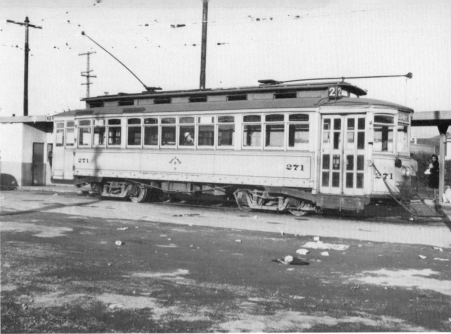

The "Lehighs"

(ABOVE & BOTTOM RIGHT) **PUR-CHASED FROM THE** Lehigh Valley Transit Co. in 1904, these 1902-built cars were used on both local lines and as trains. No. 280, seen at the Richmond yard, has couplers, applied in 1920, to haul trailers. **E.R. Mohr** No. 281's crew poses at the refinery in Richmond. **Randolph Brandt**

(TOP RIGHT) **ONE LEHIGH** survived after the others went to scrap in 1935. No 271, with lengthened platforms, was used as both a local car and Westbrae shuttle car and was saved from the torch by the Bay Area Electric Railroad Association, which still operates it at the California Railway Museum, Rio Vista Junction. It is seen at the Ashby terminal during World War II.
Brian Thompson

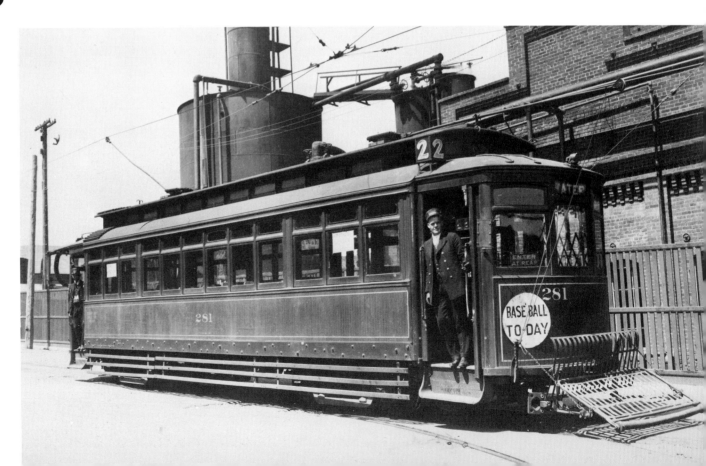

(LEFT) **THERE'S A DEFINITE** Los Angeles look to car No. 411, one of the former Eastshore & Suburban cars acquired by Key System in 1912 from that Richmond streetcar system. This is probably an official photo taken after completion of modification (such as diamond roller pantograph for use on Key's Traction Division lines), at Emeryville Shops.

E.R. Mohr Collection

(BELOW) **ANY LAD WOULD BE** honored to pose with the crew of such a fine electric railway car! No. 425, another former Eastshore & Suburban car, displays its elegance—note that fancy glass in the upper window sash! Photo was taken on the Leona line when it was identified as the "K" route.

E.R. Mohr Collection

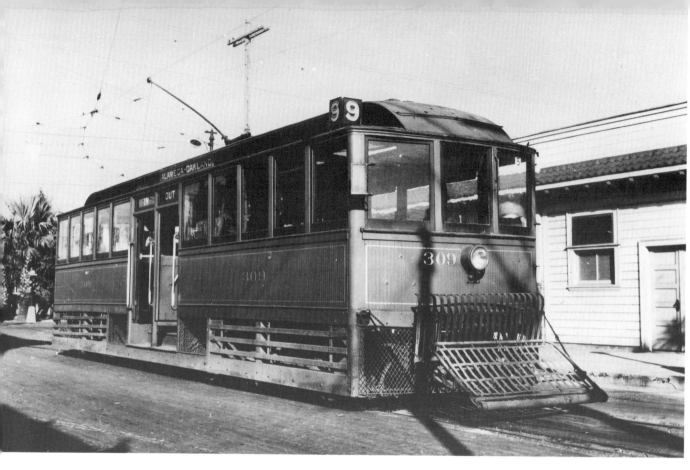

(LEFT) **AN EARLY CENTER-ENTRANCE CAR,** No. 309 was one of the "Kelly" cars built in the company shops in 1905. W.F. Kelly was the company's General Manager, and suggested the design. It is seen in the community of Alameda.

Mark Effle Collection

(BELOW) **THE CONDUCTOR STANDS** next to No. 396 ("v" of the motorman's collar and tie can barely be discerned inside the middle front window) in Berkeley. It was one of a 1911 order that comprised the system's first "Pay-As-You-Enter" cars.

Charles A. Smallwood/ Magna Collection

SWAYING ALONG on the S-curves of the No. 4 line, No. 960 stops for a snap alongside two cloth-top flivvers, in 1927, in Berkeley.

Randolph Brandt Collection

CARPENTERS' SKILLS AND HANDSOME DESIGN were combined to produce the fine cars shown at left and below, which were constructed at the company shops in 1909. Cars were modified to run in multiple unit in 1911 and performed suburban service on Hayward, Grove lines and the Key Division. In 1930 they became one-man, single-unit cars and all were scrapped by 1939.

E.R. Mohr Collection

NO. 363 POSES on the No. 1 Alameda (Santa Clara Ave.) line. This car ran through World War II but survived only briefly under the National City Lines regime.

Randolph Brandt Collection

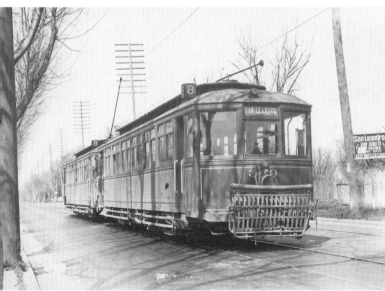

AT SAN LEANDRO'S city limits, No. 349 and mate are ready to change direction. Sign at right warns those entering the city to slow to 10 MPH and close their mufflers! **Randolph Brandt Collection**

DOWN BY THE STATION, on a cold, wet, wintry day in February 1941. Amtrak is 30 years in the future and S.P.'s 16th St. Station has two streetcar lines and the outer Harbor bus line. Twin Coach No. 12 (left) is one of the tiny buses known locally as the "cooties."

Warren K. Miller

(LEFT) No. 344 is Hayward-bound, at Castro Valley Junction. **L.J. Ciapponi**

(RIGHT) It's a fact that two cars would not clear on this curve! No. 351, stripped of its winged Key System shield by the new management, uses this unusual trackage. **E.R. Mohr**

88

Long Gone

JUST ABOUT EVERYTHING in this picture has vanished, including the wide-top Hudson on the right. We are viewing 12th Street between Clay and Jefferson, in Oakland, in February 1941. No. 385 still had its tongue and groove wood dash—a rarity by this time. **Warren K. Miller**

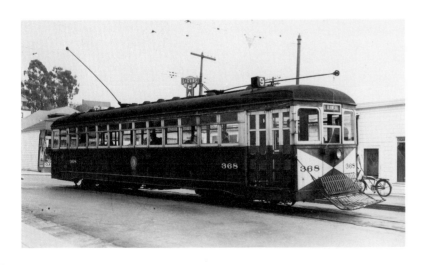

(LEFT) **NO. 368 MODELS** the East Bay Street Railways green and cream livery of the mid-1930s.
Mark Effle Collection

Multi-Track Crossing

TURNING THE CORNER AT Grove and Adeline was rather a spectacular maneuver for a No. 3 streetcar. Since the line ran parallel to both Southern Pacific's electric suburban tracks and East Bay Transit's "big brother" F line rails (making a grand six-track panorama), southbound car No. 362 made lots of "clunkata clunkata clunkata" sounds on its way across. From all the activity in this November 1940 photo, this is probably Big Game Day at Berkeley. Patrons of the F train in the distance transfer to waiting K line 900s on Alcatraz Ave. **Warren K. Miller**

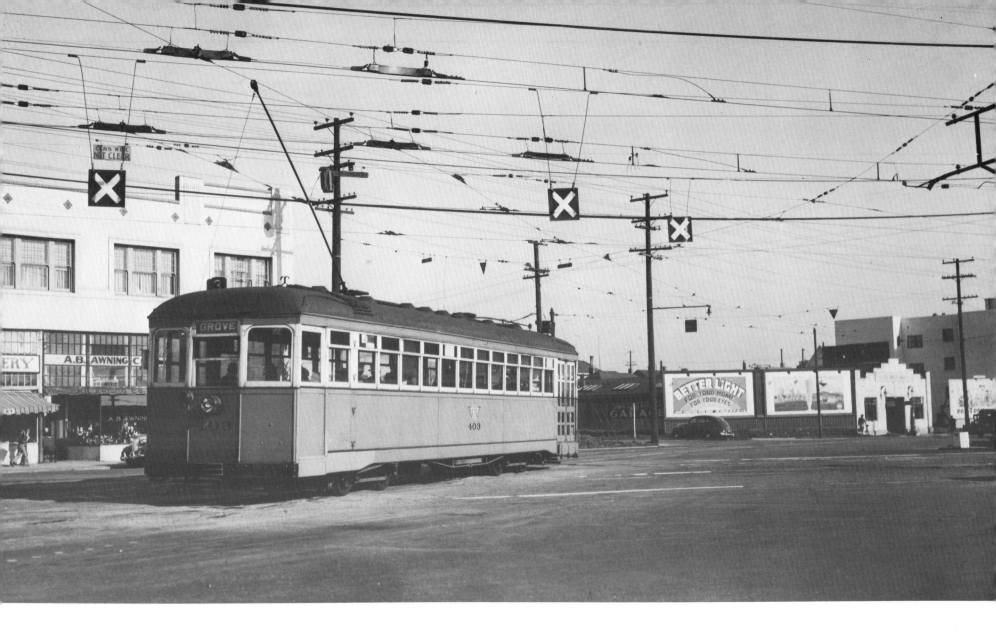

THE CAMERAMAN steps back across the S.P. tracks and aims in the other direction, toward Grove, as another southbound No. 3 car trundles across the many diamonds. Note the large wooden breakers in the trolley wire crossing to prevent the spectacle of a 600-volt-wired car contacting 1200-volt power.

Warren K. Miller

IT'S MARCH 24, 1917, on Oakland Ave., Oakland, as "brass hats" inspect brand-new streetcar No. 717. For the record, they are W.R. Alberger (former company Vice-President and General Manager), F.A. Richards (representative of builder American Car Co.), J.P. Potter (former company Vice President and Supt. of Transportation), Samuel Carwen (President, American Car Co.) and George H. Harris (former company General Superintendent, Chief Engineer and General Manager). **Robert A. Burrowes Collection**

WHAT A HOMESITE! Trolley cars from your doorstep to downtown Berkeley; a 50-foot frontage lot for as low as $95! This early-day (probably around 1920) view is at Cragmont, a neighborhood in the hilly part of Berkeley on the D (later No. 7) streetcar line. Sounds good, but what were they paying per hour that year? **Randolph Brandt Collection**

(BELOW, LEFT) **THEY LIKED CARS NO. 701-720** so well that the Emeryville Shops built center-entrance trailers 750-759 in 1918. This is not a case of copying, since the shops had built the first powered car, No. 700, in 1916. This pair of trailers is being pulled north on San Pablo Ave. by one of the 460-465 series, four-motored cars.
Roger Ciapponi Collection

(BELOW) **SIDE VIEW OF** trailer No. 757 is at 23rd and MacDonald yard in Richmond, circa 1920. This official company view was probably taken by W.E. Gardiner, who captured the essence of the Key's vast domain for many decades.
E.R. Mohr Collection

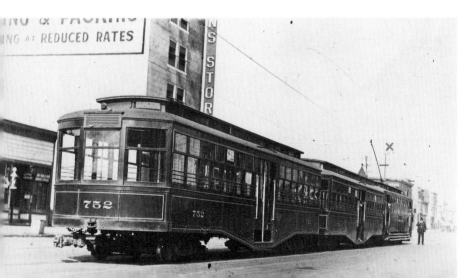

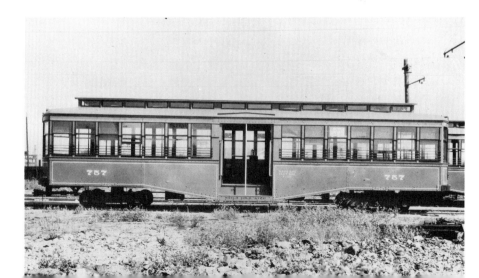

93

HARD TO BELIEVE this is the same kind of "700" shown on previous pages, but it is, after being extensively rebuilt. Obviously the original center-entrance design required a two-man crew and when the company finally won its fight to convert to one-man streetcar operation, in 1930, a big remodeling program was undertaken. End doors were cut in, the center entrance and deck roofs were removed. This left a rather low arch roof, and produced a more rakish appearance.

94

(ABOVE) **TRUNDLING THROUGH DOWN-TOWN OAKLAND,** No. 702 is on a No. 11 line assignment.   **Mark Effle Collection**

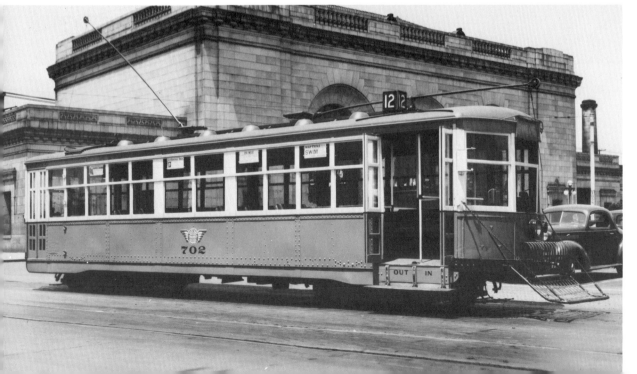

AT 16TH AND WOOD, a No. 12 car awaits passengers from Southern Pacific trains (both steam-hauled long distance trains and the big red electrics) at SP's 16th Street edifice, in the late 1930s.   **Mark Effle Collection**

AT PIEDMONT AVENUE, No. 11 car 716 will soon return to downtown Oakland. It bears the East Bay Street Railways green and cream livery in this mid-1930s view.

E.R. Mohr Collection

(BELOW) **THE END OF STREETCAR SERVICE** was very, very near as No. 702 rested at Central Car House on November 1, 1948. It has lost its East Bay Transit shield but retains the pre-National City Lines colors. The final car ran early in the morning of November 28th.

Warren K. Miller

TWENTY OF THESE handsome streetcars were built in the company shops from 1918-1920. Nos. 800-818 would see many years of service. No. 800 is shown here, as built, at the Emeryville complex.

E.R. Mohr Collection

WHEN CONVERTED for one-man use in the early 1930s, the 800s were modified in their door arrangement and by removal of the clerestory roof, the two most obvious changes in this World War II-era photo (note Army and Navy uniforms), at Shattuck Ave. and University, in downtown Berkeley.

Mark Effle Collection

ABOUT TO CROSS the "Red Trains" tracks, No. 944 takes on passengers on E. 14th St. at Melrose. S.P.'s San Leandro line crosses here. The No. 1 streetcar line had been cut back from Hayward to 105th Ave. by 1940, when this view was taken. The tiny Twin Coach at right is on the High St. line to Alameda. **Warren K. Miller**

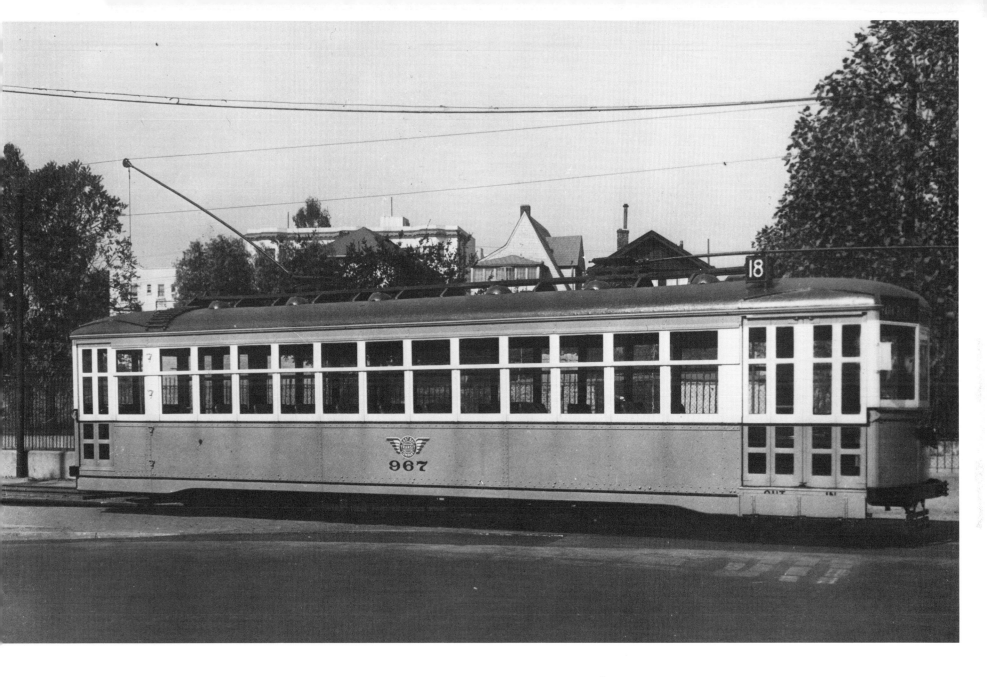

(FACING PAGE) **A COMPANY VIEW** shows the beauty of freshly painted No. 921, at Emeryville Shops, about 1927. The livery is Key System Transit Company's orange and cream.
E.R. Mohr Collection

KEY'S ULTIMATE STREETCARS were these handsome lightweights built by the American Car Co. from 1923 to 1925. The 95 cars were all-around workhorses, capable of operation on any line, either one-man or two-man, and in two-car trains or singly.

(ABOVE) By the East Bay Transit Company years, a yellow and white scheme adorned the cars and the back doors were permanently sealed. The No. 18 route was Lakeshore-Park Blvd. **A.C. Transit**

FROM DOUBLE TO SINGLE track. No. 992 turns onto Telegraph from Bancroft Way, in Berkeley.

NO. 925 TAKES ON PASSENGERS at Central Car House, E. 18th St. and 3rd Ave.

Twilight Years Gallery 1946-48

LEAVING THE F Line alignment on Adeline, No. 4 car 910 turns onto Shattuck Ave. en route to Oakland. S.P. kept a piece of its former Berkeley line track for freight service (the spur crossing Key tracks in foreground).

A FINE BROADSIDE SHOT OF No. 938 on the 5 line, at W. 7th St. and Pine Sts., Oakland.

All photos this page: E.R. Mohr

FROM 1946 UNTIL the end of streetcars in 1948, some cars wore the Key System Transit Lines yellow-green-white "fruit salad" colors, like No. 970.

Denzel C. Allen, Jr.

(FACING PAGE) **IMPRESSED** with the Brill demonstrator on exhibit at a transit conference, Key's president had it shipped to Oakland. The little car only ran two years before joining the "dead line," along with ex-Southern Pacific "dinkeys" (see behind No. 1150).

L.J. Ciapponi/Randolph Brandt

FINAL HOURS. No. 912 nears the end of its career on November 27, 1948, the last night of service on the No. 5 line. **E.R. Mohr**

ROLLING ALONG THE private right-of-way at 15th St., No. 981 has a standing load in this 1948 view. Two blocks behind is Central Car House.

E.R. Mohr

(ABOVE) See page at left.

(UPPER RIGHT) **CALLED "DINKEYS"** by the locals when Southern Pacific introduced them in 1912, they were smaller than the giant Red Trains, but a lot mightier than most city streetcars. Key purchased some of them in 1930 for local service, but retired them by 1933. This is the only known shot of one in service.

B.H. Ward/Mark Effle Collection

(BELOW) **LIKE MANY OTHER** streetcar systems, Key bought a batch of Birney Safety Cars; cars 1 to 25 arrived in 1920. Here No. 19 lays over on Park St. at San Pablo Ave., in March 1937. All were scrapped by 1940.

Warren K. Miller

(BELOW) **IT'S NOT A BUS!** This tiny Twin Coach lightweight experimental streetcar was tested on the Key but after a mishap was not used again.

E.R. Mohr Collection

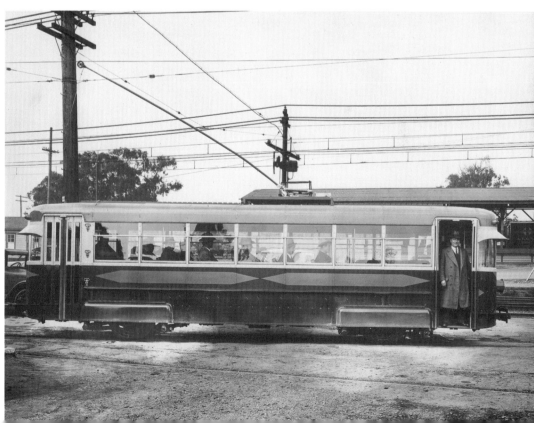

FENDER UP and pole reversed, a two-car Alcatraz train waits for the next load from the through train on Adeline before it heads east to College, sometime in the 1920s.
Randolph Brandt Collection

NON-REVENUE RAIL CARS

CONNECTING UP THE OVERHEAD wires where the new Richmond Shipyard Railway met up with the old IER (Southern Pacific) Ninth St. line, line car No. 1218 does its part for the war effort in this January 13, 1943, view. Five days later revenue service commenced.

Mark Effle Collection

They Created . . .

. . . And They Destroyed

BAM, BAM, BAM, BAM, BAM went the five pavement breaking hammers of car 1019 as it broke up paving around streetcar tracks during the removal of local rail lines in the late 1940s. **Mark Effle Collection**

Steam in Electric Territory

A STEAM LOCOMOTIVE was an oddity on such a "pure" traction line as the Key System. No. 4 performed many switching duties until its sale, in 1944, to the Modesto & Empire Traction Co. **L.J. Ciapponi/Roger Ciapponi Collection** (LEFT, MIDDLE) No. 4 is joined by electric locomotive No. 1000 at the Key Pier approach, in 1937. **Charles Smallwood/Magna Collection**

(LEFT, BOTTOM) **HEADING A CUT** of Santa Fe outside-framed box cars, Locomotive No. 1000 awaits its switching crew at the Emeryville complex. **Mark Effle Collection**

A DENIZEN OF THE SHOPS, Key's little shop switcher No. 1215 shoved cars on and off the transfer table on which it is shown at the Emeryville facility. **Mark Effle Collection**

Locomotives

STEEPLE CAB Locomotive No. 1000 hauls along a string of box cars near 32nd & Louise, not far from the Emeryville Shops, in the 1930s. There were a few on-line freight sidings. **L.J. Ciapponi**

LOCOMOTIVE NO. 1001, retained for occasional maintenance-of-way assignments, was photographed at the Bridge Yard in 1956. **Jim Walker**

NOT MUCH IS KNOWN of this tiny flat motor. A couple of workmen pose on No. 1217 in the early decades (it was gone by 1929). **Randolph Brandt Collection**

RESCUING DEAD KEY SYSTEM trains was the job of this impressive-looking Wrecker, No. 1011. Equipped with both a pantograph and trolley poles, its most distinctive feature was the siderods between axles. It is shown on the transfer table at Emeryville Shops.   **Paul Darrell/Magna Collection**

(BELOW) **TO ASSIST DISABLED CARS** on the multi-voltage bridge railway, the California Toll Bridge Authority acquired this self-propelled gas rail car from the Northwestern Pacific. It began life on the Dan Patch Lines in Minnesota. View at left shows MW-01's front end, and at right is the rear end.   **Both: Mark Effle Collection**

SMOOTHING OUT the rough spots on tracks of the Eastbay Transit Company in 1939, rail grinder No. 1020 awaits a sideways journey on the Emeryville Shops transfer table. **Warren K. Miller**

TIME OUT FOR A SANDWICH as a lineman pauses aboard Line Car No. 1201 at the Oakland Bridge Yard in July 1939. The car's profile shows definite evidence of its origin, in 1895, as a steam railroad coach on the California Railway. **Mark Effle Collection**

(ABOVE) **OIL SPRINKLER** No. 1220 was home-built by a Key System predecessor to spread its contents along rights-of-way. Note Sacramento Northern car stored at the Key System shop complex. **Magna Collection** (RIGHT) Nattily attired motormen check out a train of Differential dump cars alongside the main line at Emeryville Shops during construction of the Richmond Shipyard Railway, in 1942. **Brian Thompson**

Fire Engine Shuttle

FIRE CAR No. 1204 had only one function. It sat against this ramp (RIGHT) at Emeryville awaiting the unwelcome news of an outbreak of fire on the pier. Should such a dreaded event take place, a fire engine from the local department would rush to the ramp and climb aboard the car (like this practice drill shown in the lower right-hand photo) for a quick ride to the scene.   **Both: Randolph Brandt**

STANDING BY for heavy track construction duties, Brown hoist crane No. 1206 sleeps at Emeryville in the later 1940s. The crane assembly not only swiveled, but also traveled back and forth on its deck (note tiny wheels). Car controls are out-of-doors on this end of the car.   **Magna Collection**

Buses, Too

THIS PHOTO STUDY of the Key System focuses primarily on its rail and ferryboat operations, but we feel obliged to let you sample its rubber-tired vehicles, since they became a major part of the fleet as rail-to-rubber conversions took place.

(RIGHT) HEAD-ON view of Twin coach No. 157, at Division 2 (45th & Pablo) in 1940. Note the golden glow headlights, mounted on an external rack—often knocked off in collisions. This Model 40 Twin was originally ordered by Peerless Stages in 1930, then resold to Key in 1936. It went for junk in 1945.　　　　Robert A. Burrowes

(LEFT) EASTBAY TRANSIT COMPANY'S second No. 1 was this tiny Twin Coach, purchased in 1930, and sold to Napa Bus Lines in 1945. It awaits assignment at Western Car House (51st & Telegraph) in April 1937.　　　　Robert A. Burrowes

(BELOW) TROLLEY BUSES almost ran on the No. 6 College Ave. local line. Key System had ordered a batch from ACF-Brill in 1946 but before delivery the company sold out to National City Lines. The first 15 languished in the Lower Yard in Emeryville after the new management scrapped TC plans, and wound up being sent to Los Angeles Transit Lines for its new trolley bus lines.　　　　Brian Thompson

ON THE LAST DAY of the 42-Garvin bus line, EBT Twin Coach (a 19-seater), poses at the sparsely settled terminal at Humbolt and Garvin, in Richmond.　　　　Robert A. Burrowes.

(BELOW) CELEBRATING DELIVERY of buses B-27 through B-40, Key System Transit Co. officials gather on Telegraph Ave. in 1928. Bus chassis were built by the Fageol Motor Co. of Oakland, and bodies were from American Car Co., St. Louis (a Key favorite when it was buying streetcars). The buses were equipped with Hercules engines. The "B" prefix means "bus," a designation later dropped.
Robert A. Burrowes Collection

(ABOVE) THIS RACY PIERCE-ARROW motorcoach poses for the company photographer when new, in 1925, at Emeryville Shops.

(BELOW, LEFT) ON THE FIRST DAY of bus operation on the San Francisco-Oakland Terminal Rys., May 21, 1921, bus No. 2 was snapped on the Chevrolet Park line (serving the recently opened Chevrolet factory in East Oakland), at 62nd & Trenor. Mr. Trenor subdivided the area, but during World War II this and other streets in the same alignment became MacArthur Blvd.
Robert A. Burrowes Collection

(RIGHT) **THIS SPIFFY MOTORCOACH** was built by Reo in 1926 and served Key for three years.
Randolph Brandt Collection

WAR-WEARY Twin Coaches had been in service 15 years when these two views (right, and below, right) were taken in 1944. Gasoline rationing and war industries kept many buses going which should have been consigned to the junk pile.

(RIGHT) **NO. 131,** a 39-passenger Model 40 Twin Coach, displays years of hard wear at the 5th & San Pablo Yard.

(BELOW, RIGHT) **TURNING NORTH** onto San Pablo Ave., No. 136 leaves the Ashby streetcar-bus terminal northbound to Solano Ave. **Both: Brian Thompson**

(BELOW) **DURING PART OF** World War II, the A line had bus service nights and Sundays. Yellow Coach Model 740 No. 813, built in 1940, was one of the substitute vehicles.
Brian Thompson

113

(ABOVE) **TRANSBAY BUS** No. 805 loads passengers at the Santa Fe bus terminal at 44 4th St., San Francisco, about 1939. Key became a tenant upon completion of the highway portion of the Bay Bridge, having inaugurated express service, in May 1937, on lines L (Richmond), N (East Oakland), and R (Hayward). These buses did not pick up passengers inside transbay rail line territory, and the fare was 30¢, versus 21¢ for a combination train-ferryboat ride. This Yellow Coach was delivered in 1938.

(BELOW) **KEY BUS** No. 609 heads north on San Pablo Ave., at Ashby, in 1942, as construction proceeds apace on the Richmond Shipyard Railway. At right, buses are parked in the former park-and-ride lot (the expected rush of motorists willing to drive partway to Oakland, then board a No. 2 streetcar failed to materialize, so with the war patronage boom, the lot was used for bus parking). No. 609 was a Model 41G Twin Coach, delivered in 1939 (G stood for "gravity suspension," a hinged-front axle which gave more play to the springs).

(ABOVE) **A GENTLEMAN BOARDS** bus No. 808 at 55th & Bancroft in March 1942, when it provided substitute service for A trains on Sundays. How about that spiffy '30 Chevrolet on the left!

All photos this page: Robert A. Burrowes

LOOKING LIKE something out of a Walt Disney production, these novel tractor-trailer trams were specially constructed for the 1939-40 Golden Gate Exposition on Treasure Island and were shown on Key System's records as the "3900 class." This service was operated by Key's National Service Co. subsidiary, which also ran restaurants, newsstands, and the coffee shops on the ferryboats.

Elephant Train

(ABOVE, LEFT) **THE STREET LEVEL** loading zone at East Bay Terminal, facing Mission St. is the site for this posed publicity photo of White No. 1042 in 1946. Span wires above are for the San Francisco Municipal Railway streetcar loop.   **John McKane Collection**

(BELOW, LEFT) **THIS 1945 WHITE** product is shown in local service on Broadway, near 12th, in downtown Oakland, in April 1956.   **Robert A. Burrowes**

(ABOVE, RIGHT) **LEAVING** the Bay Bridge, O bus No. 1042, inbound from Alameda, turns at Essex and Folsom en route to the San Francisco terminal, May 1956.   **Robert A. Burrowes**

(BELOW, RIGHT) **WESTBOUND** on the lower deck of the Bay Bridge, O bus No. 1055 was snapped from an eastbound Key train in July 1956.   **Robert A. Burrowes**

TWO HUNDRED FIFTY ONE White Motor Co. buses were purchased by Key System from 1941 to 1946. The first 95 were bought to provide new bus routes over portions of what had been Southern Pacific's Interurban Electric Railway "red train" network, abandoned in 1941. These units had actually been ordered by Pacific Electric Railway, another SP subsidiary in Southern California, for its own bus conversion program, but when SP found its eastbay rail abandonment plans stymied by Key System's inability to obtain replacement buses in time, the railroad told White to deliver the buses to Key. White did, and the "Red Trains" of the bay area were replaced.

POPPING OUT OF A BOXCAR, (LEFT) One of Key System Transit Lines' 1946 44-passenger Twin Coaches makes its debut in Emeryville. Other just-arrived coaches of the 20 1200-series are in the background. Most new buses were shipped across country in this fashion. (RIGHT) No. 1201, "flagship" of the series, poses for a publicity still. All were sold to the Omaha & Council Bluffs Street Railway in 1951.

BOTH: John McKane Collection

ONE OF KSTL'S 60 Mack buses, No. 2559 was one of 10 bought second-hand from Pasadena, Calif., City Lines in 1948. The 41-passenger bus passes a building on Market, between 20th and 21st, in Oakland that was the birthplace of Pacific Greyhound Lines. The building became PGL's shop until operations moved to San Francisco.

Robert A. Burrowes

FORD MOTOR COMPANY'S contribution to public transit, the Ford Transit bus, was to be found in the Key System stable. Forty-one of these small vehicles were purchased from 1944 to 1946. No. 1513 is seen at Division 2 bus yard in 1950, the same year they were all disposed of.

Robert A. Burrowes

116

Last But Not Least — the GMC

OUR FINALE on Key System buses is devoted most appropriately to the General Motors diesel bus, which replaced one streetcar line after another, and finally did in as well the five transbay rail lines. Almost immediately after taking over management of the East Bay transit system, National City Lines did the expected by ordering a fleet of GM buses. Of the total of nearly 300 ordered between 1946 and 1958, one giant block of 160 arrived in 1947.

(ABOVE) No. 1843 turns at Beale and Folsom, in San Francisco, in service on the N transbay line, in January 1956.

(ABOVE, RIGHT) **QUITE A RIDE** could be had by boarding this line 43A bus, at Bancroft and Dutton, in San Leandro, for a trip to Solano Ave., north of Berkeley. Photo taken July 1955.

(RIGHT) **THIS SPORTY COUPE** was used on the Key System Transit Lines for shuttling supervisors and other personnel.

All photos this page: Robert A. Burrowes

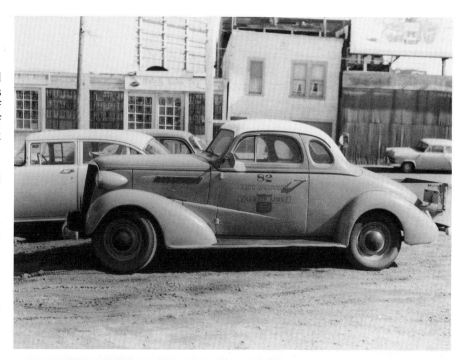

Key Potpourri

CENTRAL CAR HOUSE, at E. 18th St. and 3rd Ave., was Oakland's local transit hub. **Brian Thompson**

THE TRANSBAY TRAINS lived at the Bridge Yard, next to the toll plaza at the Oakland end of the bridge from San Francisco. **Roger Ciapponi**

AT LEONA, motorman and photo/historian L.J. Ciapponi takes his own portrait, in the mid-1930s. **L.J. Ciapponi**

THE YOUNG MEN'S CHRISTIAN ASSOCIATION building is the backdrop for this view of No. 374, on the Telegraph Ave. line in the 1910s. **Randolph Brandt Collection**

THOSE WHO RODE the Key System trains in the 1950s will recall the jarring ride and the rolling motion, which resulted from deteriorating track. This F train "rolled" a bit too far on a piece of rough track, causing the horn of one of its pantographs to hook the trolley wire and pull it down. While electricians take apart the shattered "pan," the conductor consults his watch to see how late he'll be getting home to supper. **Denzel C. Allen, Jr.**

Parting View

ILLUSTRATING KEY SYSTEM'S capacity to carry crowds is this view of football fans transferring to Key buses for the shuttle to Memorial Stadium at the University of California, downtown Berkeley on a Fall Saturday in the early 1950s.   **Denzel C. Allen, Jr.**